UNSTOPPABLE IF...

For Henry & Chris,

Enjoy 2002!

love from Steve x

for Heather

Also by Steve Bell
Bell's Eye: Twenty Years of Drawing Blood
If...Bottoms Out
The If...Files

Steve Bell and Brian Homer
Chairman Blair's Little Red Book

UNSTOPPABLE IF...

Steve Bell

methuen

1 3 5 7 9 10 8 6 4 2

Published in 2001 by Methuen Publishing Ltd
215 Vauxhall Bridge Rd, London SW1V 1EJ

Methuen Publishing Limited Reg. No. 3543167

A CIP catalogue record for this book is available from the British Library

ISBN 0 413 75990 3

Text by Steve Bell and Brian Homer

Designed by Brian Homer and Jim Deaves

Printed and bound in Great Britain by St Edmundsbury Press Limited, Bury St Edmunds, Suffolk

Contents

Contents

The Story So Far…

July 1997

Labour had just won its biggest ever landslide victory. The Tories were in total disarray. John Major had resigned as leader, taken off the Pants of Power and gone away to watch the cricket.

Disgruntlement was seething in the Shires. The natural party of government was now the knackered party of opposition. So it was that a lot of country people, whose interests had been thoroughly neglected for the last eight weeks, got together to put the case for the countryside with a massive demonstration in Hyde Park in favour of the right to rip foxes into small pieces. The Countryside Alliance was born. Toffs, yokels and stars of stage and screen, including John Major lookalike Jeremy Irons, rallied to the cause and descended on the capital…

On the March

Only the Countryside Alliance knew and understood the countryside. They held it in trust for the nation (despite the fact that they'd screwed the food chain and were planning to plant genetically modified crops everywhere). Two right wing Tory MPs, the omnivorous Nicholas Soames and the late, vegetarian, animal - loving Alan Clark were enthusiastic, if somewhat confused supporters.

14.7.1997

Monkey Box

New Labour started to show how caring it was by announcing the good news that, very soon, everyone would experience the benefits of getting a pension on the open market.

21.7.1997

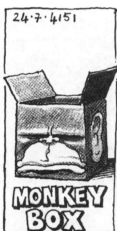

11

Sheep Wha' Hae

Devolution was in the air. "Selkie Poo" is another way of saying "Seal shit". Dolly the famous cloned sheep was developed and born in Scotland. A "teuchter" is a low class highland peasant.

28.7.1997

13

Business Links

Putting shares in a blind trust was de rigeur for politicians with business links wishing to avoid sleaze allegations. New Labour introduced a completely new approach to drugs by appointing a "drugs Czar."

4.8.1997

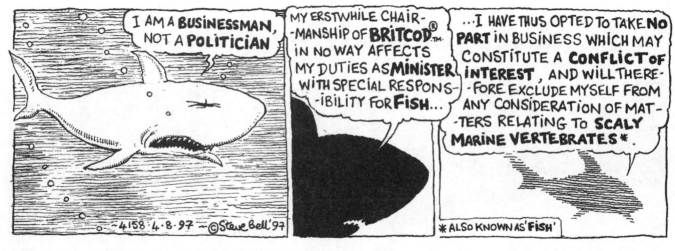

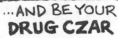

Fish Tribute

Who could explain the outpourings that followed the death of Diana? Prudence the penguin was caught up in the mass hysteria.

8.9.1997

17

Corinthians

Only three months after the election Blair's curiously messianic side began to show.

15.9.1997

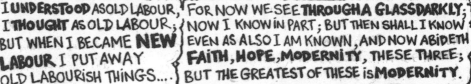

Panel 1: WHEN I WAS **OLD LABOUR**, I **SPAKE** AS OLD LABOUR,

Panel 2: I **UNDERSTOOD** AS OLD LABOUR, I **THOUGHT** AS OLD LABOUR; BUT WHEN I BECAME **NEW LABOUR** I PUT AWAY OLD LABOURISH THINGS....

Panel 3: FOR NOW WE SEE **THROUGH A GLASS DARKLY**; NOW I KNOW IN PART; BUT THEN SHALL I KNOW EVEN AS ALSO I AM KNOWN, AND NOW ABIDETH **FAITH, HOPE, MODERNITY**, THESE THREE; BUT THE GREATEST OF THESE IS **MODERNITY**.

SNAT

© Steve Bell 1997

Panel: MIXED IN A **BOWL OF HILLS** WITH WATER AND **DRIED FRUIT** ROLLED ON A BOARD OF DARK AND **VARNISHED WOOD**...

Panel: PROVEN IN THE RAIN THEN **BAKED** BENEATH FULL SKIRTS AND A **STOVEPIPE HAT**...

-18·9·4171-

Panel: DAMP, GREEN AND **SLIPPERY** YOUR MOLTEN RIVERS CHOKED BY **BRAMBLES** AND **OLD SHEEP**

Panel: **LOWERING** IN YOUR FASTNESS PROUDLY, IN THE MIST ALL **ANCIENT PASSION** SPENT A **WELSH VOLCANO**

© Steve Bell 1997

Panel: AND I SAW A **NEW HEAVEN** AND A **NEW EARTH**...

~ APOLOGIES TO ST. JOHN ~   © Steve Bell 1997
19·9·4172

Panel: ...FOR THE FIRST HEAVEN AND THE FIRST EARTH WERE PASSED AWAY; AND THERE WAS **NO MORE SEA** AND **NO MORE SOCIALISM**......

Panel: ...AND I HEARD A GREAT VOICE OUT OF HEAVEN SAYING: "**I AM THE FATHER, THE SON AND THE ZEITGEIST**...."

Panel: "...**MODERNITY** IS OUR **SPIRIT** AS IT IS THE **SPIRIT OF AN AGE*** **NEW LABOUR NEW HEAVEN**."

*T.B. 9/9/97

Discreet Triumphalism

The honeymoon was over for some as the colleagues, including Sylvester Stallone, gathered in Brighton for the Labour Party conference. Famous American pop artist Roy Liechtenstein chose this moment to die.

29.9.1997

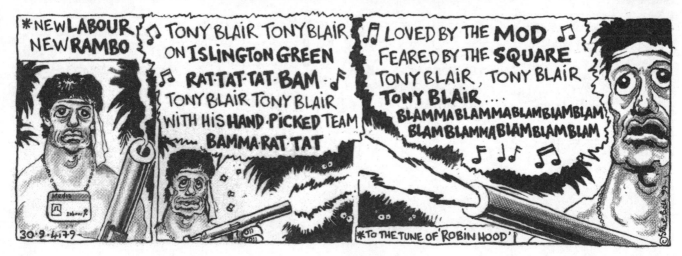

SUDDENLY.... LICHTENSTEIN'S CLOGS BLAZED INTO LIFE...

POPP!

© Steve Bell 1997 - 1.10.4180 -

HE FOUGHT THE **HARDENED LEFTIES** IN THE METHODIST CENTRAL HALL THEY **SNEERED** AT HIM AND LAUGHED ABOUT HIS **EARS** — 2.10.4181

THE BEAST OF **COMMON OWNERSHIP** HE PROMPTLY PUT TO DEATH AND **KICKED** THOSE LEFTIES OUT ON THEIR **REARS**.... © Steve Bell '97

TONY BLAIR TONY BLAIR ON **ISLINGTON GREEN** TONY BLAIR TONY BLAIR WITH HIS **HAND-PICKED TEAM** **LOVED** BY THE **MOD** **FEARED** BY THE **SQUARE** TONY BLAIR TONY BLAIR **TONY BLAIR** .....

THE PEOPLE'S FLAG IS **PALE TURQUOISE** IT FLUTTERS OVER GIRLS AND BOYS

3.10.4182 - © Steve Bell '97 -

OUR POLICIES ARE **VERY FEW** AND SUBJECT TO A TIGHT **REVIEW**

NOW **DI HAS DIED** WE'RE ALL BEREFT WE'RE CARING SHARING BUT **NOT LEFT**

SO CROSS YOURSELVES AND **BOW YOUR HEADS** GOD BLESS THE CITY **FUCK THE REDS**

Celebrity Breakup

In their unending search for media coverage it had become a cliché for celebrities to announce their breakup and Wally the Whale was no exception.

20.10.1997

Education, Education, Education

More bad news for those who thought they'd elected a progressive government – Baroness Blackstone, one of David Blunkett's junior ministers made the case for undergraduates paying fees, a measure that few could recall seeing in the election manifesto.

3.11.1997

DID YOU KNOW THAT, ON AVERAGE, GRADUATES EARN **25%** MORE THAN NON-GRADUATES?

...AND I THINK WE CAN ALL AGREE THAT COSTS SHOULD BE SHARED **MORE FAIRLY** BETWEEN THOSE WHO BENEFIT...

...THEREFORE IN THE INTERESTS OF EQUALITY AND JUSTICE, SENS-IBLE STUDES AND GLAD GRADS SAY: "**MORE FEES PLEASE!!**"

FRE EDU

PROGRESSIVE TAXATION-NO THANKS

QUESTION: WHAT WELL KNOWN PROFESSION HAS A NECESSARY PREPONDERANCE OF **GRADUATES** WHO ARE CRYING OUT FOR A SPECIAL DEFERRED **TAX HAMMERING** AFTER THEY GRADUATE???

I DON'T KNOW... IS IT **PARK KEEPERS?**

NO.

VENTURE CAPITALISTS?

NO.

DRUG BARONS?

NO

DRUG TSARS?

NO, I'LL GIVE YOU A **CLUE...**

EDUCATION! EDUCATION! EDUCATION!

TEACHERS!

CORRECT!

SO, GORDON, AS WE KNOW THAT **TEACHING** IS A CHRONICALLY UNDERPAID PROFESSION, HOW WILL IT COPE WITH THE **FLOOD**, I BEG YOUR PARDON, **DELUGE** OF **NEW TRAINEES...**

...WHEN THEY DISCOVER THE **FABULOUS EXTRA DEBT BURDEN** THAT AWAITS THEM AFTER THEY GRADUATE?

IRON CHANCELLOR

I BELIEVE IN **QUALITY TRAINING**, AFTER ALL, IT WAS A TEACHER WHO TAUGHT ME TO **READ**; IT WAS A TEACHER WHO TAUGHT ME TO **THINK**; IT WAS A TEACHER WHO TAUGHT ME TO TALK OUT OF MY **ARSE**. THAT'S WHY I BLAME THEM, INCIDENTALLY...

25

Breaking News

A committee of the great and good, led by Lady Elspeth Howe, expressed concern at the effects of children's exposure to a diet of comics and cartoons. Revelations about President Clinton's wayward member led directly to another confrontation with Saddam Hussein. The week climaxed with Formula One racing chief Bernie Ecclestone getting back the million quid he'd donated to Labour before the election, after severely embarrassing the government over the question of tobacco sponsorship.

10.11.1997

A Fast One

The Bernie Ecclestone story ran and ran and gave the first hint that New Labour's squeaky clean image was becoming tarnished.

17.11.1997

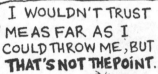

The Sweetex Gallery

The Turner Prize caused more controversy. Monsieur L'Artiste boldly stepped in.

24.11.1997

26·11·4210·

WAAA! **SHARKY BODFLUX TRINA SPUTUM** ▨ ▨ **MAKING BABIES IN A TANK** AUTUMN SEASON AT THE SWEETEX GALLERY

© Steve Bell 1997

WAAA!

RESONANT.... PIVOTAL....

© Steve Bell 1997 · 27·11· 4211·

POOO! **PABLO BODFLUX- SPUTUM** VIDEO INSTALLATION ▨ AUTUMN SEASON AT THE SWEETEX GALLERY

...NEW... RADICAL... COMPELLING...

© Steve Bell 1997 · 28·11· 4212·

GLUG! **BODFLUX SPUTUM BRITPACK** PRIVATE VIEW

SHARKY BODFLUX! TRINA SPUTUM! AH **LURVE** YOUR SHEURGH!!

AH **LURVE** YOUR BÉBÉ! AH **LURVE** YOUR PHILOSOPHIE! "WORQUE 'ARD! PLAY 'ARD! 'OOANQUE 'ARD!"

AH **LURVE** THE PIVOTAL WAY YOUR ART MAKES **PRECIOUS-NESS** ITS SOLE **RAISON D'ÊTRE!!**

ART IS WHAT ARTISTS DO (DOO)

Hot Stuff

World leaders gathered in Kyoto to make 'progress' on reductions in pollution to counteract global warming. To Socks's consternation Bill Clinton acquired a little brown dog.

8.12.1997

IS IT A BIRD?

IS IT A PLANE?

WHEEEEEEE

HEY, NO, LOOK, Y'KNOW - ®™ IT'S CONCRETE GNOME!

ETHICS TO YOU, JIMMY!

CRUMP

© Steve Bell 1997

HEY TONY - I REALLY LOVE YOUR CONCRETE GNOME... ...EXCUSE ME ONE MOMENT...

I WAS ELECTED AS CONCRETE GNOME; I SHALL GOVERN AS CONCRETE GNOME.

© Steve Bell -1997-

PFRROONT

I'VE BEEN THINKING OF GETTING A DOG, BUT A CONCRETE GNOME LOOKS LIKE A REAL NEAT IDEA!..

GET A GNOME - HE'S ALMOST AS INTELLIGENT AS HE THINKS HE IS, HE'S CLEAN AND HE'S NO SOFT TOUCH FOR GYPSIES!

HE'S CUTE, BILL. DOGS SUCK - GET A GNOME!

LISTEN SOCKS - DON'T BE UPSET... THE REASON I'M GETTING A DOG IS THIS:

THERE ARE 54 MILLION DOG OWNERS IN THE USA AND I WANT THEM ALL TO LOVE ME AND DEFLECT ATTENTION FROM PENISGATE!

YOU COULD HAVE HAD A GNOME, YOU JERK!

THE AMERICAN PUBLIC DON'T RELATE TO GNOMES, SOCKS - GNOMES ARE SOME KIND OF WEIRD BRITISH PERVERSION..

FOLKS LIKE DOGS BECAUSE THEY'RE SEXUALLY INCONTINENT YET CUTE - KINDA LIKE ME!

PAH!! I HOPE IT SHITS IN YOUR JOGGING SUIT!

© Steve Bell 97

33

Seasonal Think Tank

'Failing schools' were to have 'hit squads' descend on them to solve their problems. Despite their massive majority, the broad mass of Labour MPs showed very scant signs of independent life.

15.12.1997

*"I'M NOT SURE ABOUT THIS **YOGA DRILL** COLLEAGUE, I MEAN—WHERE'S IT LEADING?"

*"TONY TELLS US THAT ONLY A TRULY **FLEXIBLE** TURKEY CAN COMPETE IN THE NEW GLOBAL MARKETPLACE..."

*"...AND DON'T FORGET THE GREAT NEWS ABOUT OUR NEW **GROOMING FACILITY**!!"

*"I FEEL FIGHTING FIT! WHAT'S NEXT ON THE **NEW TURKEY AGENDA**?"

*"IT'S A BEAUTY TIP FAVOURED BY FORMER P.M. MARGARET THATCHER — "IT **MUST BE OK** THEN""

*—"IT'S CALLED THE **ELECTRIC BATH!** —YIPPEE!!" — ©Steve Bell 1997

*—"I THINK WE'VE ENCOUNTERED A **SETBACK**. —WHAT'S THAT??" 4227·18·12

*"OWING TO SIBERIAN-STYLE **WINTER WHITE-OUT** CONDITIONS IN CONJUNCTION WITH THE STRENGTH OF THE **POUND**..."

—"WE'RE NOT **SHIFTING OFF THE SHELVES** AS RAPIDLY AS WE'D PLANNED. SOME BELT TIGHTENING MAY BE NEEDED — YOU MEAN—WE **PLANNED** THIS?"

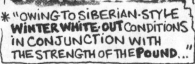

Socks on a Mission

Socks's jealousy at Buddy the little brown dog reached fever pitch. Bill stepped in to aid peace negotiations in Northern Ireland.

22.12.1997

Socks Helps Out

Socks experienced great difficulty in finding common ground among the warring parties. Meanwhile tensions were beginning to show between the Prime Minister and the Chancellor of the Exchequer.

14.1.1998

39

The President's Pecker

President Clinton apologised to the US people for his misbehaviour…

26.1.1998

Face Down

...and by some strange and mystical connection, it was time to stand up to Saddam Hussein again and send in the bombers.

3.2.1998

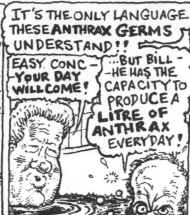
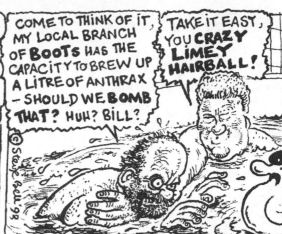

C-Men

UN General Secretary Kofi Annan expressed reservations about Bill's aggressive tendencies. Monica Lewinsky's semen-stained dress was the big story across the world.

23.2.1998

Gordie Brown is in

Gordon Brown's spending plans were not quite as generous as they would seem. There was much talk of 'Action Zones' and 'Social Exclusion' but not a great deal of actual money. Harriet Harman led the struggle against feckless single mothers who were a drain on Treasury resources.

2.3.1998

WITH APOLOGIES TO CHARLES M. SCHULZ

IS THIS A HEALTH ACTION ZONE?

- 4·2·4263 -

IS IT AN EMPLOYMENT ACTION ZONE?

DID YOU SAY SOMETHING TONY?

MAYBE IT'S AN EDUCATION ACTION ZONE?

NO - DID YOU SAY SOMETHING? HARRIET?

IT'S A SOCIAL EXCLUSION UNIT, ISN'T IT?

- ©Steve Bell 1998 -

LET ME JOIN YOUR SOCIAL EXCLUSION UNIT PLEASE?

- 5·3·4264 -

APOLOGIES TO CHARLES M. SCHULZ

GORDIE BROWN - -ARE YOU PREPARED TO SEEK OUT THE SOCIALLY EXCLUDED...

...AND EXHORT THEM TO IMPROVE THEIR LIVES WITHOUT THROWING MONEY AT THEM??

YOU BET!

©Steve Bell '98 -

THEN GO HOME AND CONTEMPLATE YOUR ESSENTIAL WORTHLESSNESS, GORDIE BROWN!

WE MUST REGENERATE THE PEOPLE.......
WE MUST RESTORE OUR HUMAN CAPITAL

6·3·4265 CHARL M. SCULZ

THE DOCTOR IS IN

WITH OUR WOWFARE TO WORK REFORMS WE WILL REMOVE THE SULLEN APATHY OF THE DEPENDENCY CULTURE....

...WILL DISMANTLE THE UNDERCLASS AND BUILD A WHOLE NEW CLASS OF PEOPLE.....

THE DOCTOR IS IN

...AN UNDERCLASS I CAN ALLOW MY CHILDREN TO MIX WITH!

©Steve Bell 1998

47

Northern Ireland Secretary Mo
Mowlam was keen to build
bridges between warring
communities of psychopaths.

9.1.1998

49

On the March Again

The Countryside Alliance staged another rally. Environment minister Michael Meacher felt their pain.

9.3.1998

The Dognut Stage

Clinton intervened in the Northern Ireland peace process in the run up to the Good Friday Agreement.

16.3.1998

WITH APOLOGIES TO SAMMY FAIN + PAUL FRANCIS WEBSTER

The Brown Family Endogenous

Tough love was the order of the day – matching the Tory spending plans with a changed rhetoric.

23.3.1998

The Compulsory Scratch Pension Show

Harriet Harman and Frank Field extolled the virtues of private pensions for all.

30.3.1998

New Thinking

Brittania was Cool and the cult of youth ruled. After the signing of the Good Friday Agreement, Tony Blair announced that this was no time for soundbites.

6.4.1998

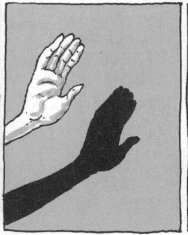

People's God and God's People

The peace process in the Middle East stumbled on.

4.5.1998

The Dead Dog Experience

World leaders attended the G8 Summit in Birmingham. Campaigners for the cancellation of Third World debt surrounded the conference centre. Brummies might want to look away now.

12.5.1998

Police Vet Camera Hospital Action

The Penguin came up with an idea for the Mother of all successful television series.

18.5.1998

POLICE VET CAMERA HOSPITAL DEATH IN YOUR FACE ACTION

...WE HAVE THE SUBJECT ON CAMERA.... COME ANY CLOSER AND I'LL EXPLODE!

-20·5·4303-

EEURRRRGHHH!!! I WARNED YOU...NNNGGH!!

BLAMMO!

©Steve Bell'98

WE INTERRUPT THIS EDITION OF TELETUBBIES TO BRING YOU IMPORTANT LIVE COVERAGE OF A PENGUIN ACTUALLY EXPLODING!

BLAMMO

RUN THAT ACTUALLY-EXPLODING-PENGUIN AGAIN!!

AGAIN! AGAIN!!

BLAMMO!

LET'S GO IN CLOSER NOW!

AGAIN! IT'S A FAKE, Y'KNOW

BLAMMO!

WE KNOW IT WAS FAKE —YOU DON'T HAVE TO TELL US!

WE UNDERSTAND THAT ANY FORM OF ACTUALITY COVERAGE IS IN FACT AN ELABORATE CONSTRUCT..

BLAMMO!

...THE IMAGERY IS OF SECONDARY IMPORTANCE. WHAT MATTERS IS THE IDEA CONVEYED – IN THIS CASE: "PENGUIN DYING ON CAMERA"

WE'VE STUDIED HAROLD EVANS AND ANDREAS WHITTAM-SMITH — —WE KNOW THAT 'LIVE DEATH' OR 'THE SNUFFMO' IS THE PUREST AND HIGHEST FORM OF JOURNALISM!!

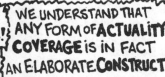

Targets

The prime target in all schools across the land was to impress Ofsted inspectors and not complain about lack of resources.

28.5.1998

Britt McCool

The Millennium Dome project was well in hand under the wise guidance of Minister Without Portfolio, Peter Mandelson.

8.6.1998

Fishball

A key part of the Glenn Hoddle's World Cup strategy as England manager was the use of a faith healer.

15.6.1998

REMEMBER – IT'S IMPORTANT TO TRY AND KEEP YOUR **FAITH UNDER CONTROL**....

CHEW CHEW

I WILL NOT STAND FOR ANY OF YOU **CROSSING YOURSELF IN HARD** FROM BEHIND.......

OMMMM

IN FACT, IN THIS TOURNAMENT, SIGNATION IN THE FIVE YARD BOX HAS BECOME A **BOOKABLE OFFENCE!**

TRY THIS SIMPLE MNEMONIC: "**SPECTACLES TESTICLES, WALLET & WATCH** – **NO WAY JOSÉ!**

-16.6.4323-

©Steve Bell '98-

WE ARE **PENGUINS!** WE ARE **'ARD!**

WE LIKE **LAGER!** WE LIKE **LARD!!**

WE LIKE SMASHING UP YOUR **BOULEVARD!**

WE ARE **PENGUINS!** WE ARE **'ARD!!**

PAUNCH

PAUNCH

18·6·4324-

- ©Steve Bell 1998-

TODAY WE HAVE OUR TRADITIONAL **GRUDGE SHOWDOWN MATCH** AGAINST THE **ALBATROSS**...

CHEW

...AS YOU KNOW, HAVING THE WINGSPAN THEY TEND TO **PLAY IT VERY WIDE.** TO COUNTERACT THIS WE HAVE TO KEEP OUR GAME AS **SHORT AND FAT** AS POSSIBLE...

CHEW

...WHICH MEANS – BEAKS UP BUMS AND REMEMBER TO **KEEP YOUR SHAPE!!**

-19.6.4325-

©Steve Bell 1998-

Business Links 2: Shagman Fuchs

Big killings were still there to be made in the city. Rock star Mick Jagger complained about his tax burden.

22.6.1998

More Fishball

England's World Cup campaign continued. Kevin Keegan provided inspiration as a commentator.

29.6.1998

Y'KNOW KEVIN, THIS VETERAN NUMBER 58 HAS A **WONDERFUL** ROLLING, STUMPING MOVEMENT....

POINK CLUMP
POINK FLAP

1·7·4333

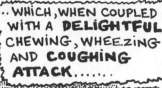

...WHICH, WHEN COUPLED WITH A **DELIGHTFUL** CHEWING, WHEEZING AND **COUGHING** ATTACK......

HRRRKKHHGGLLTUI!

...MAKES HIM A FORCE TO BE RECKONED WITH ON A FISHBALL FIELD.

THAT'S ALL VERY WELL BRIAN, BUT **TELL ME**...

©Steve Bell 1998

FIRSTLY— WILL THE **QUALITY OF THE BALLS** SIT UP FOR HIM AT THIS LEVEL? AND SECONDLY, AM I A **BUBBLEHEAD?**

WHAT'S SPECIAL ABOUT THIS BOY, APART FROM HIS AGE AND HIS **WOODEN FLIPPER**...

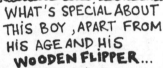

POINK POINK
CLUMP FLAP

©Steve Bell 1998 - 2·7·4334 -

...AND HIS **PIPE** AND HIS TASTE FOR **PIES**...

...IS HIS FANTASTIC ABILITY TO **CHANGE DIRECTION**......

...THAT'S WHAT DEFENCES JUST DON'T LIKE HAPPENING TO THEM AT **THIS QUALITY** OF THE LEVEL OF THE BALLS

WELL BRIAN, WHAT I FEEL IS NEEDED AT **THIS STAGE** OF THE GAME......

3·7·4335 -

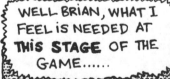

...IS A **BABBLING BUBBLEHEAD** AND LET'S FACE IT...

©Steve Bell 1998

...WE HAVEN'T HAD A **BABBLING BUBBLEHEAD** AT THIS LEVEL OF THE COMPETITION SINCE, WELL, **ME**.....

...AND LET'S FACE IT — I SNOGGED **MARGARET THATCHER!**

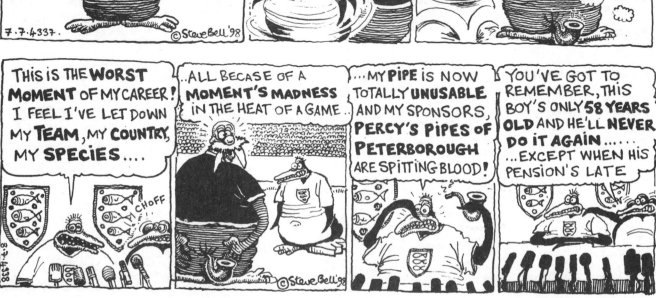

76

Ministry of Walkies

The government planned to use private money to sort out transport. John Prescott took the lead, ably assisted by the newly ennobled Trotskyist firebrand Gus Macdonald.

3.8.1998

Penis Head Cult

More controversy in the Church of England over gay and lesbian clergy.

10.8.1998

81

Madame T'atchere

Margaret Thatcher sat for an official portrait.

7.9.1998

Bill Says Sorry

President Bill Clinton apologised to the American people for his sexual indiscretions as independent prosecutor Kenneth Starr probed further into the details.

14.9.1998

John, Woy and Paddy

John Major got an important job at last and the Lib Dems were in negotiation with New Labour over proportional representation.

21.9.1998

The Third Way

There were several meanings to the Third Way, at least three for each way.

28.9.1998

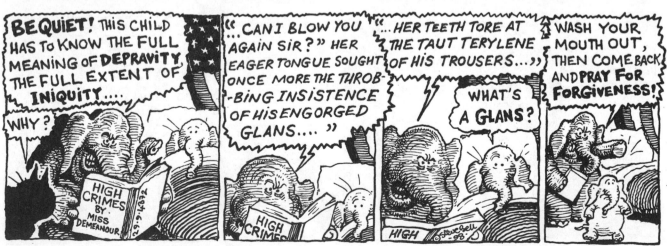

Losing the Plot

Sometimes you were forced to ask: "What's it all about then, this cartoon?". Sometimes it was difficult to think of a reply. Adverts for something called the "Alpha" movement suddenly appeared, as if in answer to our prayers.

12.10.1998

91

In the Lords

Augusto Pinochet was arrested for crimes against humanity whilst on an anger management course at a Harley Street Clinic.

19.10.1998

Margaret Thatcher and Sir Edward Heath shared the stage and some uncomfortable looking armchairs during an unconvincing display of party unity at the Bournemouth conference.

8.10.1998

She's Barmy!

Each time she appeared in public the ex-Prime Minister seemed more and more crazed.

26.10.1998

Royal Letters

After a visit to Transylvania Prince Charles expressed mild impatience to get on with "The Job". Prince Philip met Mary McAleese, the new Irish President.

9.11.1998

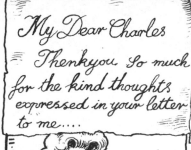

My Dear Charles
Thankyou. So much for the kind thoughts expressed in your letter to me....

SKWEE SKWIT

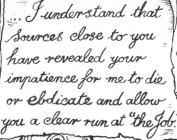

...I understand that Sources close to you have revealed your impatience for me to die or abdicate and allow you a clear run at "the Job."

SCRIT SCRIT SCRIT

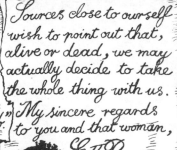

Sources close to ourself wish to point out that, alive or dead, we may actually decide to take the whole thing with us.
My sincere regards to you and that woman,
E II R

SCRAT SCRAT

Fark! Fark! Fark!!

©Steve Bell 1998

THIS IS AN **HISTORIC MOMENT**, MRS McALEESE...

...I MEAN WE'VE HAD OUR **DIFFERENCES** IN THE PAST, BUT LET'S FACE IT, **UNDER THE SKIN**....

©Steve Bell '98

...**YOU MICKS** ARE ALMOST AS THICK AS **I AM!!**

TOK TOK

Dear Pa
You bastard! All I ever wanted was a kindly word...

SCRIT SCRAT

...a spot of Tender Loving Care and a few fields of organic turnips to manage, while I settled down with a good woman...

SCRIT SCRIT SCRIT

©Steve Bell 98

All I ever got from you was cold showers and brutal injunctions to sow my wild oats before I took on the business of expanding the Empire, like a real man.

SCRAT SCRAT

Just remember this for the future: I'd rather make Mandelson my official Consort than keep you 'n the payroll,
your affectionate son
Charles

SCRIT SCRIT SCRIT

Dangerous Vegetables

Margaret McDonagh, General Secretary of the Labour Party came down hard on signs of independent thought within the party.

16.11.1998

Panel 1: Hmmm mmmm mmmm mmmm mmm mnn — COULD YOU MUMBLE MORE SLOWLY, SIR?

Panel 2: ARE YOU **TALKING TO THE MEDIA?** YOU KNOW THE RULES ABOUT TALKING TO JOURNALISTS! — MMMM MMM

Panel 3: MISS McDONAGH — I KNOW THIS TURNIP — 'E'S A **JOURNALIST** 'IMSELF!! — HNNM MMM

Panel 4: THEN MAKE SURE YOU **DON'T TALK TO YOURSELF** EITHER!!

THANKS TO MARTIN

Panel 5: VEGETABLE PARTY MEMBERS WILL NOT TALK TO **JOURNALISTS**. WHAT THE **VEGETABLE PARTY** DOES IS A MATTER FOR THE MEMBERSHIP AND THE **MEMBERSHIP ONLY!!**

Panel 6: ...DO I MAKE MYSELF CLEAR. ANY QUESTIONS? — HOW WILL WE KNOW WHAT'S GOING ON IN THE PARTY IF WE HAVE **NO** CONTACT WITH JOURN- -ALISM?

Panel 7: EVERYTHING WILL BE EXPLAINED IN THIS MONTH'S EDITION OF **'NEW HAPPY VEGETABLE'** — new Labour new Britain — **new** Happy **VEGETABLE** — BOILING OR SLICING? OPPORTUNITY FOR CHOICE

Panel 8: HAVE YOU SEEN MY PIECE IN THIS MONTH'S EDITION OF **'NEW HAPPY VEGETABLE'**

Panel 9: IT'S A HEART-WARMING STORY OF HOW I'D LIKE TO BE BOILED, MASHED, CREAMED, TURNED INTO A **'DUCHESSE'**...

Panel 10: ...AND CONSUMED BY ONE OF THE **QUALITY**, WHO WILL THEN BE MOVED TO USHER IN AN ERA OF **PEACE** AND **SOCIAL JUSTICE**...

Panel 11: WHAT DO YOU THINK OF **THAT?** — ISN'T THAT LAST BIT RATHER ON THE **RADICAL** SIDE??

Cruising on the Common

Welsh Secretary Ron Davies made a serious error of judgement on Clapham Common at midnight.

23.11.1998

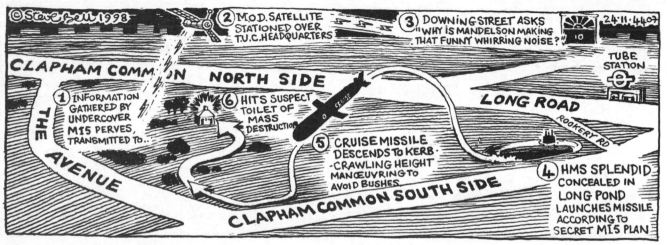

The Stoats Must Die

The government announced the end of the right of hereditary peers to sit in the House of Lords, and still the stoat holocaust continued.

30.11.1998

The Blue Shadow

William Hague's debating style matured.

7.12.1998

107

Shooting Grice

14.12.1998

Socks in Rat Alley

Things looked bad for Bill Clinton as Kenneth Starr homed in on the details of his sexual indiscretions. Things looked even worse for Socks, the most powerful cat on earth.

18.1.1999

The Blue Carrot

He came to clean up British politics and ended up having lunch with Lord Irvine of Lairg.

1.3.1999

115

Banana Wars

The Americans tried to obstruct the European Union's banana imports from the Caribbean .

8.3.1999

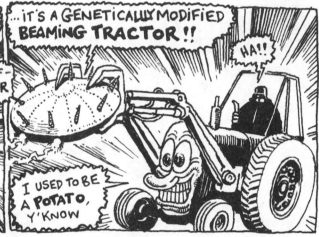

Deep Sheep Answers Your Queries

15.3.1999

DEEP SHEEP ANSWERS YOUR QUERIES....

15·3·4456 — © Steve Bell '99·

Dear Deep Sheep where does cork come from?
yours sincerely
Concerned of Droitwich

BAAAAAAAARRK

Dear Deep Sheep What's the *first* syllable of the title of T.S. Eliot's drama about Thomas A Becket?
yours
Johnny B. Interesting Soho

MEH·EH·EH·EH·EHR ·DER IN THE CATHEDRAL

Dear Deep Sheep What do you call an elongated trough wherein one can immerse one's entire body?
yours sincerely
J.P. Marat

16·3·4457 — © Steve Bell 1999·

BAAAAAAAAAATH

Dear Deep Sheep Can you think of another name for a massive shed used for agricultual purposes?
yours
Seth Hogswain Gloucestershire

BAAAAAAAAAAAAAARN

119

Banana Wars II

More banana pranks from the heroic duo of European Commissioners, Leon Brittain and Neil Kinnock.

22.3.1999

Think Fish

Nato began bombing Yugoslavia in response to Slobodan Milosevic's attempt to ethnically cleanse the majority Albanian population from the Serbian province of Kosovo. An American 'Stealth' bomber was shot down. Socks kept an eye on the bigger picture.

29.3.1999

Twelve Days That Didn't Shake the World

It was the first anniversary of the Good Friday Agreement in Northern Ireland and progress towards a peace settlement was grindingly slow. War Leader Blair and his Chief of Defence Staff Sir Charles Guthrie stressed the need to remove violence from the equation.

5.4.1999

Evil Hog of Death

European countries struggled to deal with Milosevic who had stepped up his programme of ethnic cleansing in response to the high altitude Nato bombing campaign. There was talk of 'ground war'.

19.4.1999

127

Fantasy Ground Force

There was even more talk of 'ground war'. The twentieth anniversary of Margaret Thatcher's accession to power was rapidly approaching.

26.4.1999

Armchair Warriors

Despite the talk of 'ground war', the reality of the air war was becoming more squalid with, amongst other things, the dropping of cluster bombs on civilian areas within Yugoslavia.

3.5.1999

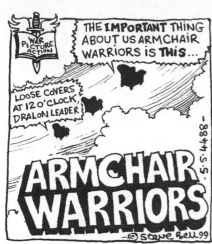

People's Crony

Plans were announced for a "new" kind of peerage for "ordinary" people.

10.5.1999

Trident in Disguise

Relations with China were strained as a result of NATO's bombing of the Chinese Embassy in Belgrade.

17.5.1999

I'M WORRIED, BOSUN, VERY WORRIED INDEED...

...THE DISGUISE YOU CHOSE—I DON'T THINK IT'S GOING TO FOOL THOSE WILY CHINESE...

TRIDENT

19·5·4498

A USED CONDOM THIS SIZE JUST ISN'T CONVINCING

BABY I LURVE IT WHEN YOU GROSS ME OUT!

© Steve Bell '99

DON'T YOU THINK A JOBBY ON THIS SCALE WILL SIMPLY ATTRACT ATTENTION, BOSUN?

-20·5·4499-

HMMM... IT MAY NOT BE DISCREET BUT STATUS AS A PROTECTED SPECIES COULD BE VITALLY IMPORTANT...

© Steve Bell 1999

YOU ASK WHY YOU HAVE TO GO THREE MONTHS WITHOUT A WOMAN ON BOARD THE BIGGEST PHALLIC SYMBOL IN THE WORLD? I'LL TELL YOU WHY, BOSUN....

-21·5·4500-

...IT'S SO THAT PEOPLE IN THE UK CAN SLEEP SAFELY IN THEIR BEDS, KNOWING THAT WE ARE SOMEWHERE, PERMANENTLY POISED, READY TO WHACK BELGRADE, BYELORUSSIA OR BEIJING...

© Steve Bell 1999

...ARMED WITH A NUMBER OF DEVASTATING INTERCONTINENTAL BALLISTIC NUCLEAR MISSILES AND A REALLY REALLY UP TO DATE ATLAS OF THE WORLD!

I Love Maddie

Aesthetically challenged Foreign Secretary Robin Cook related in a very special way to US Secretary of State Madeleine Albright.

24.5.1999

I ♥ MADDIE

ALL THIS BILLING AND COOING HAS GIVEN ME A **STIFFY!**

ME TOO, YA LITTLE GINGER HAIRBALL!

YOU TOO?! YOU REALLY ARE A **REMARKABLE WOMAN!!**

OURS IS A **REMARKABLE UNION**, ROBIN....

YESSSS!!

26·5·4·503

© Steve Bell 1999

I ♥ MADDIE

C'MON ROB... GET OFF YOUR **ASS!**

WE'VE GOTTA SHOW THE WORLD THERE'S **NO SPLITS!**

MY **GAHD!** WHAT HAPPENED? YOU'RE EVEN **UGLIER** THAN USUAL!

WHAT DID YOU SAY?? I WAS MILES AWAY DOING MY EARLY MORNING **YOGA**

27·5·4·504

© Steve Bell 1999

I ♥ MADDIE

MADELEINE — WOULDN'T YOU AGREE THAT IN THE WORLD OF **INTERNATIONAL RELATIONS**...

...IT'S A **POSITIVE ASSET** TO BE PERCEIVED AS **RECKLESS, DANGEROUS, ERRATIC, EVEN MAD?**

I LOVE IT WHEN YOU TALK DIRTY! LET'S GO BACK TO MY PLACE AND **GET ETHICAL!**

SIGH!

28·5·4·505

© Steve Bell 1999

137

War on the Roof of the World

India and Pakistan shaped up to each other again.

31.5.1999

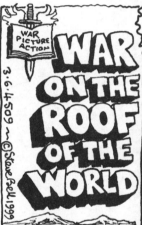

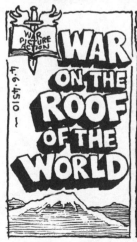

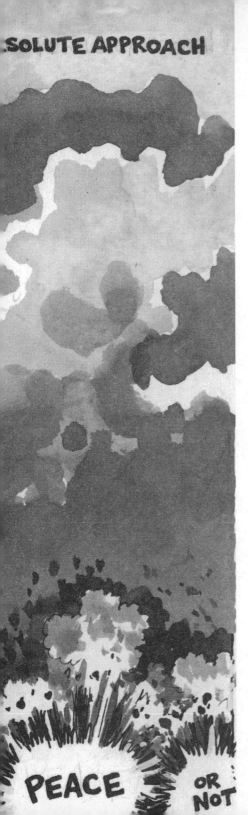

Victory in Kosovo seemed to bring out the inner War Leader in Tony Blair.

9.6.1999

The Return of the Armchair Warriors

After pressure from the Russians, the Serbs finally pulled out of Kosovo. The Russians embarrassed NATO by seizing control of the airport in Pristina.

14.6.1999

143

Viva Nato!

Nato forces rolled into Kosovo. Lucan Hardnose, lifestyle journalist, son of Harry, was with them all the way.

21.6.1999

WHERE ARE YOU NOW, YOU **PILGERS**, **PINTERS** AND **ALIS**?? I LISTEN TO THE **PEOPLE**, EVEN THOUGH I CAN'T UNDERSTAND A WORD THEY'RE SAYING...

GET OUT OF YOUR DRAWING ROOMS - YOU SHOULD BE **HERE NOW**, AT MY FEET, **WITH THE PEOPLE**, LOVING THIS **SIMPLE TANK**......
.... IT'S **HUMBLING**!

WE BRING **PEACE**, WE BRING **JUSTICE**, WE BRING **LIBERTY** WE BRING **TRUTH**!! THIS IS JUST SO **FUCKING HUMBLING**; LUCAN HARDNOSE, WITH **KFOR**, NORTH OF PRISTINA...

WHAT'S THE **DIFFERENCE** BETWEEN A **SERB** REFUGEE TRAILER AND AN **ALBANIAN** REFUGEE TRAILER? I'LL TELL YOU.....

...THE ALBANIAN TRAILER IS **FULL** OF **PEOPLE**, THE **SERB** TRAILER IS FULL OF **FRIDGES**. REMEMBER THIS. SERB REFUGEES ARE THE MORAL EQUIVALENT OF **ELECTRICAL CONSUMER GOODS**

...THIS IS **LUCAN HARDNOSE**, LIVING IN THE LOVE OF THE COMMON PEOPLE, WITH **KFOR**, NORTH OF PRISTINA!!

THIS IS **LUCAN HARDNOSE**, WITH **KFOR**, NORTH OF PRISTINA, LOOKING DIRECTLY INTO THE **EYE OF THE BEAST**....

VUG VUG- VUG VUG

EYES THAT HAVE MEASURED THE DEPTHS OF **ATROCITY**, JAWS THAT HAVE TASTED THE FRESH **BLOOD** OF INNOCENT CHILDREN, THE SMILE, THE DISEASED **RICTUS** OF UTTER MORAL DETACHMENT...

IF ONLY I HAD SOME WAY OF LETTING HIM KNOW **I'M** ALBANIAN AND **YOU'RE** THE **SERB DEVIL DOG**!

YOU COULD TRY SHAGGING HIS LEG?

Irish Dancing

Northern Ireland Secretary Mo Mowlam presided over more talks with David Trimble and Gerry Adams as the marching season approached.

28.6.1999

Lest We Forget

Bill Clinton got involved in Northern Ireland again as Buddy the dog reached maturity.

5.7.1999

149

The Jobsworth of the Year Awards

This was dedicated to the little people.

12.7.1999

...AND IN THE CATEGORY OF 'SNIVELLING JOBSWORTH', TONIGHT'S AWARD WINNER IS:

1999 GOLDEN JOBBIE — SNIVELLING JOBSWORTH OF THE YEAR

ANDREW MACKAY, SHADOW SPOKESMAN ON NORTHERN IRELAND AND FORMER ESTATE AGENT!

MR MACKAY—WHERE WERE YOU WHEN THE GOOD FRIDAY AGREEMENT WAS BEING SIGNED?

I WAS ON MY HOLS! ARF ARF ARF!!

GOLDEN JOBBIE

LAZE 'N' GELM, THE WINNER OF THE 1999 LIFETIME'S ACHIEVEMENT JOBSWORTH IS...

1999 GOLDEN JOBBIE — LIFETIME'S ACHIEVEMENT JOBSWORTH

...LORD JENKINS OF HILLHEAD! FORMER HOME SECRETARY, CHANCELLOR OF THE EXCHEQUER, FOUNDER OF THE SDP, EUROPEAN COMMISSIONER, MENTOR OF OUR PRESENT PRIME MINISTER...

1999 GOLDEN JOBBIE

...AT THE END OF THE DAY THERE WAS NOONE ELSE IN THE CONTEST, YOU POMPOUS, CLARET-SOAKED, INESTIMABLY OVER-RATED OLD FART!

I SHALL TWEASURE MYSELF!

FINALLY, THE NOMINATIONS FOR SUPER JOBSWORTH OF 1999, THOSE WHO HAVE MADE THE ULTIMATE SACRIFICE TO PRESERVE THEIR OWN JOBS...

LORD GODALMIGHTY, WHO GAVE HIS ONLY BEGOTTEN SON IN ORDER TO PRESERVE THE CULT OF HIMSELF....

WILLIAM JEFFERSON CLINTON, WHO SACRIFICED AN INDETERMINATE NUMBER OF IRAQIS OVER THE LAST 12 MONTHS TO PRESERVE HIMSELF IN OFFICE...

JOHN PRESCOTT, WHO GAVE HIS OWN BALLS ON A PLATE TO STAY AT NUMBER TWO... AND THE WINNER IS...

We Like it Damp!

The Foreign Secretary Robin Cook visited Argentina. The Penguins journeyed back to their roots.

19.7.1999

153

The Solar Eclipse

11.8.1999

Panel 1: DURING THE BRIEF PERIOD OF **TOTAL DARKNESS** THE **STARS** COME OUT ONE BY ONE...

BAAAAARRGH!!

Panel 2: GREETINGS **VAL DOONICAN!!**

HULLO THERE!

Panel 3: WELCOME **TANIA THE GOAT** FROM 'EMMERDALE'...

BLEEAURRGH!

BABABA BUMBUM BUM BABA...

Panel 4: FINALLY — A TANTALISING MOMENT OF UTTER **COSMIC OBLIVION,** OF LIGHT AND LIFE **EXTINGUISHED,** WHAT WE CALL THE **MANDELSON MOMENT!**

Panel 5: 1-8-45414

WO! HUP! LI'L DOGIE!!

Panel 6: **HOWDY STRANGER!** GUESS YOU WANNA KNOW WHY I'M A-RIDIN' THIS HERE **APALOOSA SHEEP...**

© Steve Bell 1999

Panel 7: ..CARRYIN' A BALLOON SHAPED LIKE **TONY BLAYER'S HAID?** I'LL TELL YA:

Panel 8: IT'S BECAUSE THE **TOADAL ECLIPSE** DONE BEEN AND GONE AND ALL THAT'S LEFT IS THE **SILLY SEASON....**

WHUSSA 'APALOOSA SHEEP'?

Panel 9: 13.8. 45415

SO, HOW WAS THE **ECLIPSE** FOR **YOU,** LI'L DOGIE?

Panel 10: AS SOON AS THE **LIGHTS** IN THE **SKY** WENT OUT, I WENT **PLUM LOCO!**

SO HOW COME YOU DON'T GO PLUM LOCO EVERY DAY AT **SUNDOWN**

© Steve Bell 1999

Panel 11: BECAUSE I'M TOO DAMN **TIRED!** IT'S PLUM HARD BEIN' A **APALOOSA SHEEP,** A-RIDIN' THE RANGE..

Panel 12: YEEHA!!

KICK

BUCK

BAAARRGH!!

THRASH

155

Project Hague

William Hague tried to look more convincing.

16.8.1999

PROJECT HAGUE

HAI!! NNNK! KRUNCH

NNNGGKK NNNK! RRR!

HAI! POP! CHOP

WAN-KO!!

©Steve Bell 1999
-18-8-9-

PROJECT HAGUE

BIG PROBLEM — BESIDE THE FACT THAT EVERYONE HATES YOU...

...OLDER VOTERS SEE YOU AS RIDICULOUSLY YOUNG WHILE YOUNGER VOTERS SEE YOU AS IMPOSSIBLY OLD!

WE'D BETTER START BY IMPROVING YOUR STANDING AMONG YOUTH. ANY IDEAS?

ALL I HAVE TO DO IS TAKE DRUGS AND STAY UP LATE!!

PHYLOSAN

©Steve Bell 99
-19-8-4-5-4-9-

PROJECT HAGUE

THIS IS GETTING DESPERATE WILLIAM!

YOU'RE GOING TO HAVE TO GROW A BEARD!

EXCELLENT! AS SOON AS MY BOLLOCKS DROP I SHALL DO PRECISELY THAT!

I'M AFRAID IT'S MORE URGENT THAN THAT! PUT THIS FALSE ONE ON!

THIS IS BRILLIANT! NOBODY'S GOING TO MESS WITH ME IF I LOOK LIKE AN OSTRICH NEST!

©Steve Bell 99
-2-0-8-7-55-

THANKS TO THE B.L.F.

157

Wholesome Gypsy Rovers

Home Secretary Jack Straw outlined the difference between bogus travellers and the genuine article.

23.8.1999

Nanny Internet

It was revealed that parental control software was blocking out any mention of Scunthorpe on the World Wide Web.

6.9.1999

The Carthorses

The TUC met for it's annual Congress in Brighton where it was addressed by the Poet Laureate and the Prime Minister.

13.9.1999

Good Ol' Chucky Bum

Charles Kennedy took over as leader of the Liberal Democrats. Charles M.Schulz, cartoonist and author of 'Peanuts' announced his retirement.

20.9.1999

GOOD OL' CHUCKY BUM
-22.9. 4558-

THE UNIVERSE IS TERRIBLY VAST...

© Steve Bell 1999

...AND THE LIBERAL DEMOCRATIC PARTY IS TERRIBLY SMALL...

APOLOGIES TO CHARLES M. SCHULZ

...BUT I FEEL NO FEAR, FOR MY FAITH IN HYPOTHECATION AND SUBSIDIARITY IS STRONG!

GOOD OL' CHUCKY BUM
-23.9. 4569-

TONY— I'VE ADMIRED YOU FOR SIMPLY AGES!

© Steve Bell 1999

I LONG FOR A SIGN THAT YOU IN SOME WAY RECIPROCATE MY FEELINGS

WAP!

WITH APOLOGIES TO SCHULZ

I THINK WE HAVE THE BEGINNINGS OF A RELATIONSHIP!

GOOD OL' CHUCKY BUM
-05.6. 542-

TONY'S LET ME HAVE EXECUTIVE FACILITIES OF MY VERY OWN...

CHUCKY

WITH APOLOGIES TO CHARLES M. SCHULZ

...WITH AIR CONDITIONING AND CLOSE PROXIMITY TO THE HEART OF THE GOVERNING PROCESS

♪ THINGS CAN ONLY GET BETT-ERR CAN ONLY GET BETT-ER-ERR... ♪

CHUCKY

100 Years of Baked Bean progress

The Labour Party celebrated its 100th anniversary at its annual conference in Bournemouth.

27.9.1999

Mr Turd Goes to Conference

The Tories debated Europe at their conference in Blackpool.

4.10.1999

MR TURD GOES TO CONFERENCE

A FRINGE MEETING OF ANGRY TURDS...

WE MUST GET **OUT** OF EUROPE!

THE ONLY SENSIBLE FUTURE IS **BOBBING** AROUND IN THE MIDDLE OF THE **ATLANTIC**...

...LOCKING OURSELVES INTO THE EUROPEAN SINGLE **EFFLUENCY** WILL ONLY **COST JOBBIES!**

HAS ANYBODY EVER TOLD YOU HOW DEEPLY UNATTRACTIVE YOU ARE?

MR TURD GOES TO CONFERENCE

WE ARE **TURDS!** WE ARE **STRONG!**

SAVE OUR STOOLS

LISTEN TO US! LEAVE US ALONE!

PHEW!

WHAT A STINKER!

LISTEN TO OUR FLIES!

BZZZT

BZZZT

BZZZT BZZZT

BZZZZT WE FIND YOU IMMENSELY ATTRACTIVE

MR TURD GOES TO CONFERENCE

WE ARE **TURDS!** WE MUST **UNITE!** GAY AND STRAIGHT, POINTED AND ROUND, LOOSE AND **FIRM**, SMELLY AND EVEN MORE SMELLY...

WE ARE **TURDS!** WE ARE **STOOLS!** WE MUST **RISE UP NOW** AND **ATTACK THE FAN !!!**

Johnny Big Pants Looks Back

John Major's memoirs, which he wrote himself, were published.

11.10.1999

...SO I SAID TO HER: "NO WAY!!"

13·10·4583

"GET OUTA MY FACE AND GET BACK TO FROM WHENCE YOU CAME!"

"I'M IN CHARGE NOW! I AM JOHNNY BIG PANTS..."

"...CAN I FETCH YOU A NICE CUP OF BLOOD?"

© Steve Bell 1999

Y'KNOW - POLITICS IS LIKE BICYCLING...

14·10·4584

...WITH THE CORRECT AMOUNT OF DILIGENT EFFORT...

© Steve Bell 1999

...YOU GET WHERE YOU WANT TO GO..

DING DING

OH YES, POLITICS IS VERY LIKE BICYCLING....

15·10·4585

...THE REAL PROFESSIONALS LIKE TO WEAR VERY TIGHT, BRIGHTLY COLOURED CLOTHING...

...THEY TAKE LOTS OF DRUGS AND HAVE THEIR FEET BOLTED TO THE PEDALS...

...AND FREQUENTLY GET FOLLOWED BY DOGS....

© Steve Bell 1999

The Minister of Walkies

John Prescott wanted to bring the benefits of privatisation to the London Underground.

18.10.1999

Reintroducing Snakes into Ireland

Peter Mandelson was back from the political wilderness after being made Secretary for Northern Ireland.

25.10.1999

William Buys a Lorry

William Hague readied himself for his campaign to Save the Pound. Unfortunately, he found it very hard to procure a truly British lorry untainted by foreign owners or parts.

1.11.1999

Grilled by Beans

Ken Livingstone went before the selection panel that was to choose the Labour candidate for Mayor of London.

8.11.1999

GRILLED BY BEANS

© Steve Bell 1999. 10-11-4603

MR LIVINGSTONE - ARE YOU **BAKED**?

I AM **FULLY OVEN-BAKED**, BUT NOT TOO MUCH.

DO YOU BELIEVE IN THE ABSOLUTE RIGHT OF **TONY BLAIR** TO SAY AND DO WHATEVER HE LIKES IN THE PROMOTION AND FURTHERANCE OF **OUR COMMON PURPOSE**, WHATEVER HE MAY DECIDE THAT TO BE?

I BELIEVE THAT **TONY BLAIR** IS A VERY ASTUTE AND EFFECTIVE POLITICIAN.

ANSWER THE QUESTION!

ARE YOU IN FACT AN **EGG**?

GRILLED BY BEANS

10-11-4604

MR LIVINGSTONE - HAVEN'T YOU BEEN DEMONSTRABLY PROVEN TO BE AN **EGG·O·CENTRIC** PSEUDO BEANISH FAKE PULSE?

I AM A **BEAN**. I BELIEVE IN **SAUCE FOR ALL BUT NOT TOO MUCH**!

© Steve Bell 1999

IT'S NO USE REPEATING SLOGANS IN A MANTRA-LIKE MANNER. THAT SIMPLY BETRAYS DANGEROUS SIGNS OF **INDEPENDENT THOUGHT**....

...FOR YOU'RE **NOT** A **TRUE VEGETABLE** AT ALL, ARE YOU, MR LIVINGSTONE?

I AM A **BEAN**! **ICH BIN EINE BOHNE**!

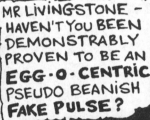 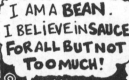    

BEAN THOUGHT

THE PANEL DECIDES

12-11-4605

THAT **LIVINGSTONE** - WHAT A **BASTARD**!!

THANK YOU CHAIR! WHAT DOES EVERYBODY ELSE THINK?

HE'S A *⊛☆✳!! PIECE OF **EGG·O·CENTRIC** *⊛✳**!

I HATE HIM!

HE'S A **GIT**!

© Steve Bell 1999

HE USED TO HAVE **FACIAL HAIR**, Y'KNOW

DOBBO'S GOT FACIAL HAIR!

THAT'S IRRELEVANT - **DOBBO** IS **APPROVED**, THAT'S ALL WE NEED TO KNOW.... ...ARE WE ALL **AGREED**?

BETTER LIVINGSTONE **OUTSIDE** THE CAN PISSING IN THAN **INSIDE** THE CAN PISSING OUT!!

WE ARE BEANS! WE LIKE SAUCE, BUT NOT TOO MUCH. HOW COULD WE DISAGREE?

179

The Morning After

Most of the hereditary peers were swept out of the House of Lords.

12.11.1999

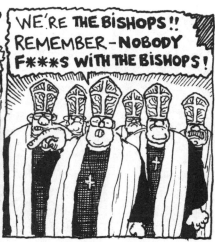

A Foecus Group

The Blair's were pregnant!

22.11.1999

182

Archer Disowned

The Tory Party's candidate for Mayor of London went down in flames after revelations about an earlier libel case. William Hague called in the Conservative Ethics Committee to investigate.

29.11.1999

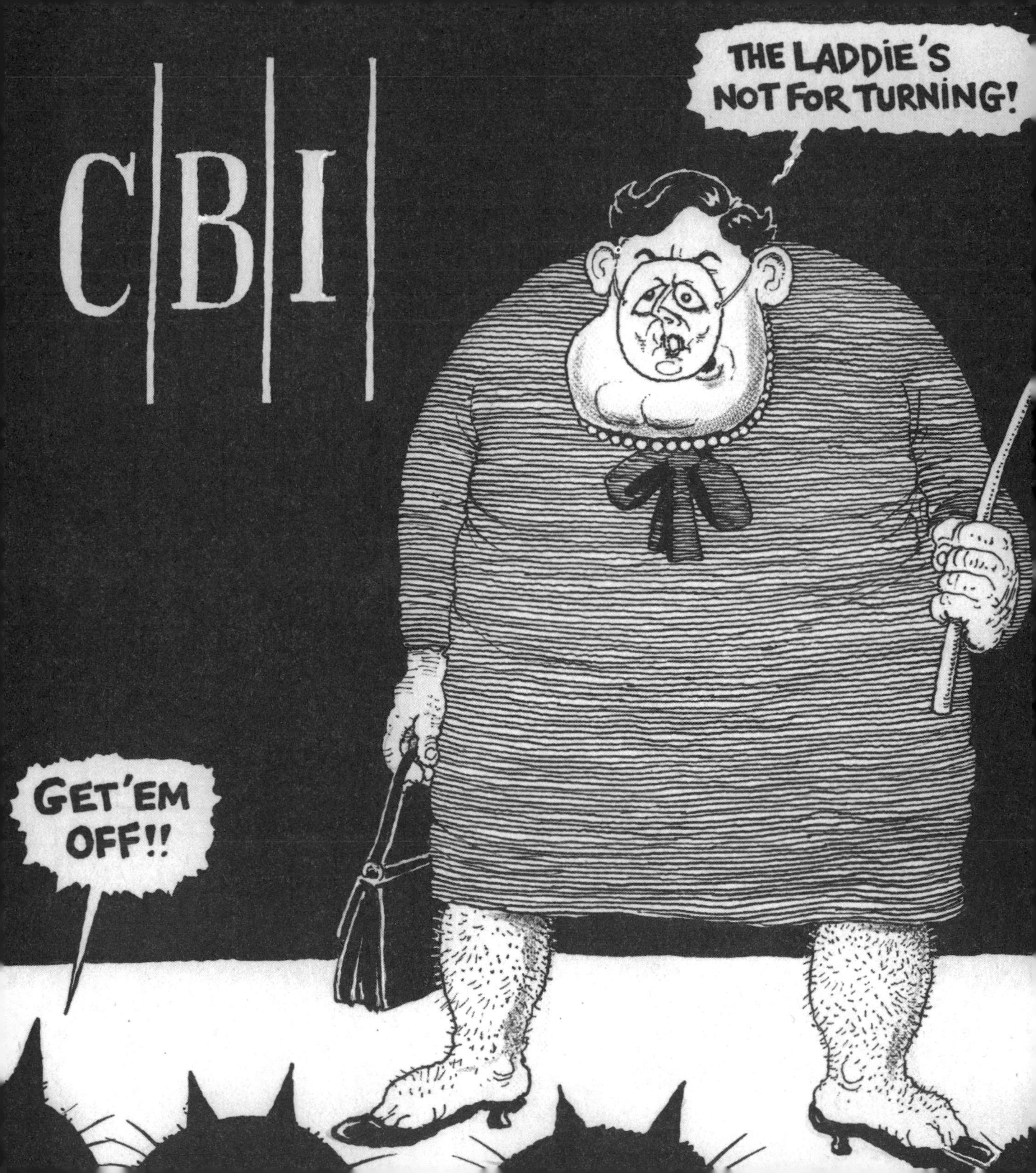
CBI
THE LADDIE'S NOT FOR TURNING!
GET'EM OFF!!

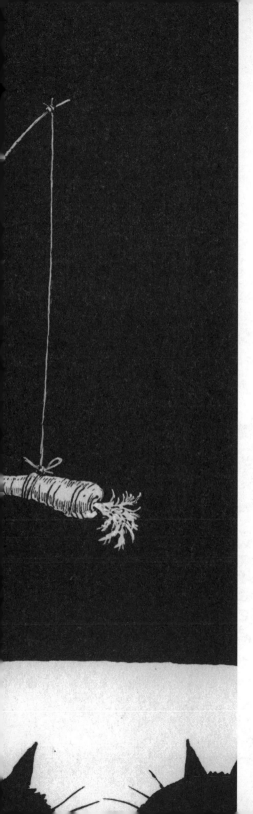

Gordon Brown impressed the CBI conference with his prudent, business-friendly credentials.

2.11.1999

How Damp Was My Sheep?

6.12.1999

HOW DAMP WAS MY SHEEP?
-8-12-4623-

CATCH UP ON THESE FABULOUS GIFT IDEAS...

...YOU'VE HEARD OF PASHMINAS...

YOU'VE HEARD OF THOSE TIBETAN SHAWLS THAT ARE SO FINE THEY CAN BE PULLED THROUGH A WEDDING RING...

NOW THE UNPARALLELED LUXURY OF THE DEEPSHEEP®-TM- QUALITY HAIRBALL

ONLY £29.99

DEEP SHEEP MERCH-O-MART
-9-12-4624-

YOU'RE NEVER ALONE...

© Steve Bell 1999 -

BAAAA BAAAA

HELLO - I'M ON A TRAIN AND IT LOOKS LIKE RAIN!

WITH THE DEEPSHEEP®-TM- BRAND MOBILE PHONE ONLY £399·99

DEEP SHEEP MERCH-O-MART
10-12-4625

GET RADICAL! THE BADGE IS BACK!

SO WEAR ONE UP FRONT!

IT'S ACTUAL SIZE!

RIGHT ON BALDY! DEFEND CLAUSE 28

ONLY £4·99

- © Steve Bell 1999 -

Whippets and Willie

Steven 'Shagger' Norris was set to replace the disgraced Archer as mayoral candidate. William Hague and his pals had other ideas.

13.12.1999

Deep Sheep in the Snow

Millenium fever gripped the nation.

20.12.1999

Millenium Crabs

The much feared Millennium Bug failed to materialise except inside Tony Blair's trousers.

10.1.2000

Granny on a Trolley

A slight spell of cool damp wintry weather caused chaos in the NHS.

17.1.2000

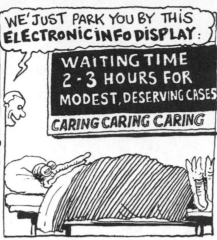

Clause for Concern

The campaign to keep the anti-homosexual Clause 28 gathered pace. In Scotland it was led by the late Cardinal Thomas Winning and bus magnate Brian Souter.

24.1.2000

Willie and Miguel

Michael Portillo got back into Parliament after a by-election in Kensington and Chelsea caused by the death of the vegetarian racial hygiene enthusiast Alan Clark.

31.1.2000

A Vacuum in My Heart

Beset with problems like millionaire ex-minister Geoffrey Robinson and the popular rejection of his favoured candidate for the post of First Minister in the Welsh Assembly, Alun Michael, Tony Blair began to betray signs of self doubt.

7.2.2000

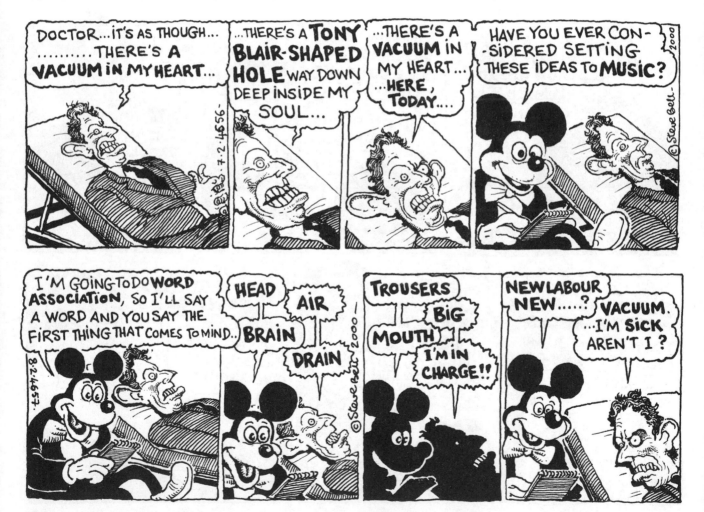

203

Endgame

The exact forms of words of a disarmament agreement in Northern Ireland was under the microscope.

14.2.2000

Londergirds Are Go!

Frank Dobson, Tony Blair's preferred candidate for Mayor of London was finding it hard going against Ken Livingstone who had threatened to quit the party to run as an independent.

21.2.2000

208

Da Number of Da Beast

13.3.2000

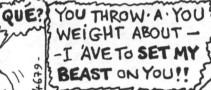

The Seekers

"Bogus" asylum seekers were under attack from the Government and the media.

20.3.2000

Over the Edge

The male menopause has unexpected consequences for the Penguin.

27.3.2000

Safe as Houses

The sale of British Nuclear Fuels is put on hold because of worries about security and the cost of clearing up nuclear waste.

3.4.2000

Mondeo Man

"Mondeo Man" was credited with voting in New Labour.

10.4.2000

Tarzan – Still Swinging

Michael Heseltine spoke out in support of "his" Dome, which was failing to attract visitors.

1.5.2000

Cock-A-Hoop

William Hague felt good about jumping on the first of a series of bandwagons.

8.5.2000

Worrying Times

The Queen opened the Tate Modern gallery in the old Bankside power station. It was an immediate success in vivid contrast to the Dome. In Scotland Brian Souter, supported by Cardinal Winning was busy organising his own referendum about the repeal of Clause 28.

15.5.2000

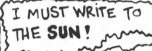

Penguin Incubation

The Penguin had problems reproducing Antarctic winter conditions in Peckham.

22.5.2000

Stella By Stealth

Dame Stella Rimington, the ex-head of MI5, wrote her memoirs.

29.5.2000

Home Secretary Jack Straw proposed sweeping new international measures to counteract football hooliganism during the European Championship Finals in Belgium and the Netherlands.

5.7.2000

To Hounds!

The hunting lobby made its case, at length, yet again.

12.6.2000

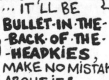

235

Rooting Out Bent Cricket

Following the Hansie Cronje betting scandal in South Africa, Sir Paul Condon was appointed to tackle corruption in cricket.

26.6.2000

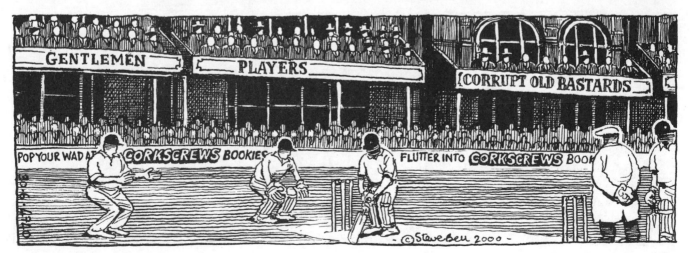

Take Me to a Cashpoint

The Government suggested giving the police powers to impose on-the-spot fines for anti-social behaviour, taking the perpetrators to a cash point if necessary.

3.7.2000

EX-TER-MIN-ATE

Lord Birt, former BBC chief, was to deploy his formidable management skills in the area of Law and Order.

10.7.2000

EV·E·RY·MIN·UTE·OF·EV·ER·Y·DAY·A **CRIME**·IS·BE·ING·COM·MIT·TED....

NEED·**MEA·NING·FUL**·**RE·SPONSE**·JAMES...

FLA·SHING·LIGHT·ON·ROOF·OF·**LI·MO**·SHOWS·BIRT·MEANS·**BUS·INESS**.

EVE·NING **ALL!**

FETCH·ME·A·**PLANK**·AND·A·KEY·TO·THE·**EX·EC·U·TIVE·WASH·ROOM**..

I·NEED·TO·**DOWN·LOAD**·AN·**IN·TER·NAL·RE·PORT**....

STOP! THIEF!...·DRUN·KEN·YOUTHS·HAVE·STO·LEN·MY·**PLUNGER!!**

THIS·TALK·OF·**CRO·NY·ISM**·MAKES·ME·**AN·GRY**....

THERE·ARE·**NO·CRO·NIES**·ON·TO·NY'S·TEAM! **CHE·RIE! DAH·LING!** MM·WAA·MM·WAA

JOHN! SO GOOD TO **SEE YOU!** MMWAA!! MM MMMWAA!!

TO·NY!! MMWAA! **MM·WAAA!** YOU·LOOK **WELL**...AND·**SO·RE·LAXED!** THOSE·TROU·SERS·MUST·BE·**E·LA·STI·CA·TED!**

The Bum on Sunday

A national newspaper "outed" alleged paedophiles on its front page.

31.7.2000

The Price o' Gas

In America the election contest between Vice President Al Gore and Governor George W. Bush of Texas was hotting up. In Britain a campaign against high petrol costs was started under the slogan "Dump the Pump".

7.8.2000

245

Fourteen Pints

In an attempt to boost his "lad" appeal William Hague, in a magazine interview, claimed to have regularly drunk fourteen pints a day while working as a drinks delivery man.

14.8.2000

YES – I'VE SHAGGED MORE BIRDS THAN **ERROL FLYNN** AND SUNK MORE ALE THAN **OLIVER REED**....

I'M A REAL **LAD'S MAN** – I'VE GOT MORE CHEST HAIR THAN **KING KONG**!...

...AND **THAT'S NOT ALL** – D'YOU WANNA KNOW SOMETHING I'VE TOLD NO-ONE ELSE...

I WAS THE NOTORIOUS **"HEADLESS MAN"**!

YOU COULD TELL THE NOTORIOUS 'HEADLESS MAN' WAS **ME** FOR SEVERAL OBVIOUS REASONS....

ONE: MY **SEXUAL PROWESS**;
TWO: MY **WASHBOARD STOMACH**;
THREE: MY LUXURIANT **BODY HAIR**;

WHAT ABOUT THE FACT THAT THE 'HEADLESS MAN' PICTURES WERE TAKEN IN 1956, AND YOU WEREN'T BORN UNTIL 1961!

IT WAS IN MY PREVIOUS **EXISTENCE** AS A FAMOUS HOLLYWOOD **SWASHBUCKLER**!

MORE ALE, WENCH! I FEEL A **SONG** COMING ON!

I'M SINGING A **SONG** IN PRAISE OF MY **DONG**!

...THE LADIES ALL THRONG.... – **MY DONG IS SO LONG!!**

Big Bottom

The reality TV show *Big Brother* was the subject of much discussion.

21.8.2000

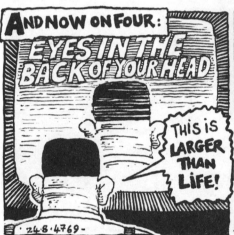

Art for Art's Sake

It transpired that, in their younger days, both the Blairs had posed for portraits in the nude.

4.9.2000

Olympic Bandwagon Jumping

11.9.2000

Vengeance of the Fat Blokes

Protests at the duty on petrol were led by an unlikely alliance of self-employed lorry drivers and farmers (whose diesel fuel is tax exempt).

18.9.2000

Baked Beans in Crisis

The Government was taken by surprise at the fuel protests.

25.9.2000

BAKED BEANS TO THE RESCUE

...AND I SAY UNTO YOU, MY BEANS — SAUCE, **BUT NOT TOO MUCH**; BE REALISTIC,....

...I **WILL NOT**, I **MUST NOT BACK DOWN** BEFORE UNELECTED FAT BLOKES...

...BECAUSE IT'S **YOU** THEY WANT FOR BREAKFAST, **NOT ME!**

NEW FARTINESS

27.9.4788.

WE ARE THE FAT BLOKES

WE EAT BAKED BEANS FOR BREAKFAST

WE ARE HUNGRY

FEAR THE WIND OF CHANGE

BOGGLER BOGGLER BOGGLER BOGGLER

BOGGLER BOGGLER

BOGGLER THROG

THROG THROG BOGGLER THROG

28.9. 4789 — © Steve Bell '00

THE BROWN FLAG

THROG BOGGLER BOGGLER BOGGLER THROG THROG BOGGLER THROG THROG BOGGLER THROG

THROG BOGGLER BOGGLER BOGGLER THROG THROG BOGGLER THROG THROG BOGGLER THROG

THROG BOGGLER THROG THROG BOGGLER THROG THROG BOGGLER BOGGLER THROG THROG THROG...

THROG BOGGLER BOGGLER BOGGLER THROG THROG BOGGLER THROG THROG BOGGLER THROG!

-29.9.4790-

SUNG TO THE TUNE OF THE RED FLAG

© STEVE BELL 2000 —

257

Tory Direct Action Society

The Tory conference centred around a series of rallies in support of farmers and fat blokes.

2.10.2000

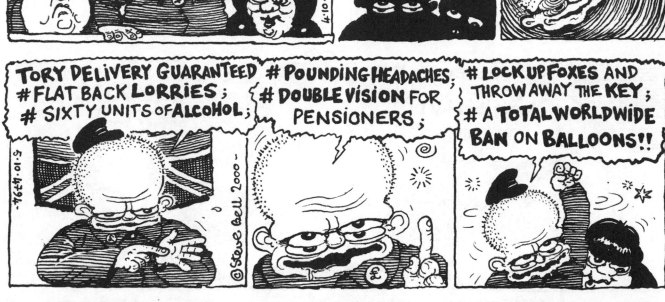

259

Splifflady

Anne Widdecombe's zero-tolerance policy on drugs was immediately undermined when colleagues in the Shadow Cabinet revealed that they had tried soft drugs in the past.

9.10.2000

Flooded

Vast tracts of the country were flooded including parts of East Sussex.

16.10.2000

Off the Rails

The high-speed rail crash at Hatfield was the direct result of failure to maintain the track since privatisation. Gerald Corbett was the chairman of Railtrack at the time.

23.10.2000

BSE: The Truth at Last

A report into BSE criticised the Tory Government's handling of the crisis.

30.10.2000

MARGARET THATCHER-HOW DO YOU PLEAD?

WE MUST PUT ASIDE THE BLAME CULTURE. IT WAS NOT I....

...THAT WAS RESPONSIBLE FOR EVERYTHING WRONG OVER THE LAST TWO DECADES. IT WAS THE TRADE UNION BULLY BOYS.....

...THE SINGLE MOTHERS; THE FRENCH; THE ALIENS WHO SWAMP OUR LAND; THE SCROUNGERS; THE SHIRT-LIFTERS; THOSE WHO WOULD DENY ME MY SHERRY OF AN AFTERNOON...

2·11·4814--.

CHOFF CHOFF   SCRUNCH SCRUNCH

© Steve Bell 2000.

CHOFF SCRUNCH SCRUNCH

PHEW! JUST AS WELL YOU REMINDED ME!

DO NOT CANNIBALISE MY REMAINS

3·11·4815·

I DON'T WANT TO GET INVOLVED IN THE BLAME GAME......

...BUT WHY CAN'T YOU STUPID *@¤‡**@※ COWS GET YOUR ACT TOGETHER ON THE MUNCHIES FRONT??

WHAT DO YOU MEAN? IT'S MAD *@¤‡**@※ SHEEP STARTED THIS WHOLE THING IN THE FIRST PLACE!

CRAP!

© Steve Bell 2000

WOOLLY MORON!

BOVINE DOLT!

IT'S COW EAT SHEEP OUT THERE!!

Back Flips

Research appeared to show that Falklands penguins would topple over backwards when RAF aircraft flew low overhead.

6.11.2000

269

Shitco Cleans Up

Problems were revealed in the service provided by private refuse collection contractors.

13.11.2000

...AS YOU KNOW, SHITCO HAS AQUIRED THE **REFUSE CONTRACT** FOR THE BOROUGH OF WARMINGTON-ON-SEA.

15-11-4823

OUR TENDER PROMISED **MORE SHIT** GATHERED FOR **LESS MONEY FOR EVER!**

FOR EVER! I LIKE THAT

TOUGH QUESTION- HOW ARE WE GOING TO DO IT?

IT'S A **SHIT- -ON-FAN MOMENT** I AGREE...

© Steve Bell 2000

...BUT BASICALLY WE **SACK ALL THE BINMEN** AND RECRUIT SMALL HAIRY CREATURES WITH **LONG TAILS**

LIFE IS **GOOD**, RHONDA- THIS **NEW JACUZZI** IS DOING WONDERS FOR MY **COMPLEXION!**

16-11-4824

YOU'RE RIGHT, RICK-THIS **HOT BOG** ®™ WAS EXPENSIVE BUT WELL WORTH IT!

© Steve Bell 00

LOOK AT **THIS** -- HAVE YOU SEEN THE NEWS?

'WALL OF SHIT' THREATENS WARMINGTON -ON-SEA

LUCKY WARMING- TON-ON-SEA I SAY!

HMMM-BUT THERE COULD BE **P.R.** PROBLEMS

HEY! 'MEA CULPA'! THE SO-CALLED **'WALL OF SHIT'** IS VERY **BAD NEWS** FOR THE PEOPLE OF WARM- -INGTON-ON-SEA

17-11 4825

YES! THE BUCK STOPS HERE AT SHITCO BUT THERE WAS A SEVERE BREAKDOWN IN COMMUNICATION WITH THE **SUB- CONTRACTORS**

WHO ARE THE **SUB-CONTRACTORS?**

THEY'RE A HIGHLY REPUTABLE FIRM OF **COCKROACHES**

COCKROACHES?

© Steve Bell 00

YES, CAN ANY OF YOU HERE **SPEAK COCKROACH?**

YOU SEE OUR PROBLEM?

NO

Club 180-309

It was discovered that some whales could live to over 200 years of age.

20.11.2000

Leader of the Free World

The "Worlds Greatest Democracy" elected George W Bush as President in a close and disputed election.

4.12.2000

It's a Crine Shame

Big-Mouth Billy Bass, a talking wall plaque, was a popular gift item.

11.12.2000

As the General Election drew nearer William Hague and Shadow Home Secretary Anne Widdecombe laid greater and greater emphasis on the need to tackle "bogus" asylum seekers by locking them all up.

15.12.00

Hail To The Chimp

George "Dubya" Bush took up the reins of power in the Unites States. All the quotes are genuine.

8.1.2001

Hands Off Our Way of Life

The hunting lobby was agitating yet again to prevent its favourite pastime being outlawed.

22.1.2001

A Pain in the Hindujas

The media were putting pressure on Blair, Mandelson and Europe Minister, Keith Vaz, over the way in which the millionaire Hinduja brothers were granted British passports.

29.1.2001

DOCTOR VAZ

I'M AFRAID YOU MAY HAVE WHAT'S CALLED...

...IRRITABLE HINDUJA SYNDROME. AS A PROMINENT LEADER OF THE HINDUJA EXPERT COMMUNITY...

...I RECOMMEND A THOROUGH EXAMINATION OF YOUR HINDUJAS OR HINDUJOSCOPY AS WE CALL IT.....

...THIS MAY TAKE A CONSIDERABLE AMOUNT OF TIME AND AN ENORMOUS AMOUNT OF MONEY!

31·1·4858 - © Steve Bell 2001

TELL IT TO ME STRAIGHT DOCTOR VAZ - WILL I LIVE?

AFTER AN EXTENSIVE AND COSTLY INVESTIGATION - I CAN STATE WITH SOME AUTHORITY THAT YOU ARE SUFFERING FROM...

...DESENSITISED, UNRESPONSIVE HINDUJAS. THIS IS EASILY REMEDIED BY A SIMPLE APPLICATION OF...

SQUARE DEAL VAZ ® -TM- BRINGS UP HINDUJAS CRISP AND SPARKLING LIKE NEW!!

1·2· 4859 - © Steve Bell 01

SQUARE DEAL VAZ

I'M NOT HAPPY, DR VAZ! I THINK YOU'VE BEEN EXPLOITING YOUR POSITION IN ORDER TO PROMOTE COMMERCIAL PRODUCTS!

MR BLAIR - ARE YOU SURE YOU'RE NOT ENTERTAINING A NEGATIVE ATTITUDE BECAUSE I IS FAT?

I'M PROUD TO BE A PROMINENT LEADER OF THE FAT COMMUNITY. I'M PROUD OF WHAT FAT PEOPLE HAVE DONE FOR THIS COUNTRY! LOOK AT HENRY VIII, WINSTON CHURCHILL, WILLOUGHBY GODDARD.....

2·2·4860

SQUARE DEAL VAZ

FOR HINDUJAS THAT REALLY SHINE

© Steve Bell 2001

The One-Eyed Trouser Snake

Peter Mandleson resigned a second time from the Government, this time over his involvement in the Hinduja affair. He was angry and feeling hard done by. Meanwhile, the Labour Party revealed a new campaigning logo.

4.2.2001

Pebbledash Man

In a bid to win the votes of the successor to "Mondeo Man", William Hague proudly revealed his election winning gambit: a new, even fuzzier haircut.

12.2.2001

Faith-Based Initiatives

The Government discovered a cracking new idea to improve "bog-standard" comprehensives.

19.2.2001

293

Contributions Please

The Lord Chancellor was criciticised for compromising his position by fundraising for the Labour Party amongst the legal profession.

26.2.2001

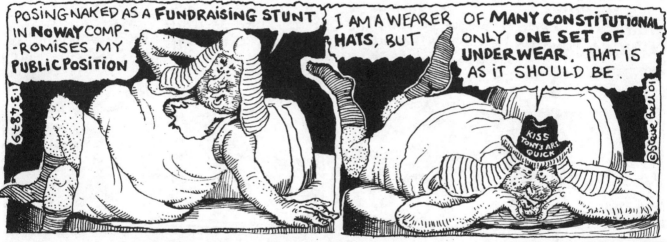

Tony Meets the Chimp

Blair was the first European leader to visit the new US President.

5.3.2001

Blame the Pigs

The rapidly escalating Foot and Mouth epidemic cut off access to the countryside and threatened to delay the expected May 3rd General Election.

12.3.2001

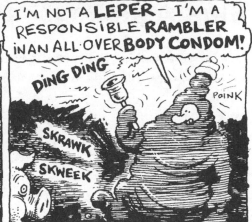

Blue Arse Day

Celebs were making arses of themselves for charity, again, while the Prince of Wales and the Duke of Westminster pledged support to farmers stricken by Foot and Mouth.

19.3.2001

The Countryside is "Open"

The Government were desperate to persuade tourists that, despite Foot and Mouth, it was still worth visiting the countryside. Blair agonised over whether to postpone the Election.

26.3.2001

Whack-A-Whale

Bored with cutting back on fossil fuel consumption, George Bush hit on a dynamic new way of saving the planet. Meanwhile, an American spy-plane crash landed in China.

2.4.2001

Poonds For Bairns

The Iron Chancellor's plans for giving all babies money for their education were not quite what they seemed.

30.4.2001

...or the Calf Gets it.

A nation that was normally only too happy to eat anything put in front of it was spellbound by a calf saved from the Foot and Mouth cull. Blair finally decided to 'go to the country' on June 7th.

7.5.2001

The Chucky Bum Express

Charles Kennedy planned to visit as many consituencies as possible.

14.5.2001

Dog Day Afternnoon

Deputy Prime Minister John Prescott was in trouble for whacking a protestor who threw an egg at him. Meanwhile William Hague was buzzing about in a helicopter called Common Sense.

21.5.2001

The Mighty Chin

Miles and miles on battlebuses took its toll of politicians, spin doctors and journalists. Elsewhere, Bob Dylan hit sixty.

28.5.2001

Werrkin' Out

As the campaign drew to a close the Labour Party began to worry that voters would stay at home in droves, which might favour the Tories. The turn-out was the lowest since 1918, but the Tories still only made a net gain of one seat.

4.6.2001

Farting for Your Country

A strange post-election malaise hung over the country as the Labour Party struggled to work out why nobody seemed to love them even though they had another huge majority.

11.6.2001

The Same Old Story So Far Again...

June 2001

Labour had just won its second biggest ever landslide victory. The Tories were in total disarray. William Hague had resigned as leader, given up all hope of even a sniff of the Pants of Power and gone off to spend more time with his back numbers of Hansard...